THREE-DAY WEEKEND

Three-Day Weekend

Poems

Christopher Blackman

GUNPOWDER PRESS • SANTA BARBARA
2024

Published by Gunpowder Press
David Starkey, Editor
PO Box 60035
Santa Barbara, CA 93160-0035

ISBN-13: 978-1-957062-12-9

www.gunpowderpress.com

For Danielle

Contents

"Time flies like an arrow; fruit flies like a banana."

—Groucho Marx

I.

Feast of St. Michael and All Angels

We stood in a crowd beneath strings of lights,
each of us moved by possibility, joined
in vague conspiracy, giving the night
the feeling that cranes could carry a camera above us,
were it all a film, to denote our scale, to denote the rush
of being in the right place at the right time—
distant terrace drums emanating from a tent on the hill,
murmurs echoing from the halls of the silent auction...
all these and other modes of bishop-approved
conviviality to celebrate Archangel Michael's victory
against the devil and his armies. I couldn't imagine
a more fitting occasion for a feast: our vices permitted
for one weekend only, as if to say "Now that I've quit
I can have one." Reason enough. Reason enough to park
at the dark side of the lot behind the Radisson
to drink for free and commemorate the occasion.
All the best things happen in parking lots—patches of turf
deposited like spurs across the skeleton of the continent
wherever people come together to read the will,
to pick up a pizza, to pawn the ring, to sleep for a night
in the kingdom of cars. So we toasted highballs
to angels and election day. We toasted to our jobs,
which called themselves "bakery-cafes" and "scoop shops,"
and all week we looked forward to the three-day weekend,
for the opportunity to be beautiful, to behave indiscriminately
in unsupervised lots, carousing and naked with the confidence
of Oliver Reed because we were all Women in Love, counting days
until the next holiday weekend appeared on the calendar
like a Wendy's in the desert appears to a thirsty wanderer
after miles of dune. And when we had eventually joined them

at the feast beneath the strings of lights, a melancholy
washed over me and I felt suddenly that I was, having been
a prince for many years, now watching the subjects wheel
a guillotine to the dais at my coronation. And as the blade dropped
I cursed the revolution for not bringing me along on the ride.

Freedom!

Even now, I worry that no pleasure
will ever rival the feeling of being sixteen
and leaving work for the afternoon,

peeling the green polo shirt from my body
and racing home to drink a beer,
or stare at the cloudless blue sky

until it flattened me beneath it
like a jump boot. I'll do almost anything
or more often, nothing, to taste

this feeling in adjacent forms, until
I'm up late weeping about the '90s and all
that they entailed—the personal computer,

the chicken pox vaccine, "No Diggity,"
and some vision for the future that began
in the basements where we gallivanted

under dim rays which always illume
occult behavior. You are in this version too:
love-drunk, leaning on the loadbearing beam

of an underground room, helping to keep
the building standing—see how love
softens? The heart becomes immune

so that no bug can afflict us like *that*
the second time. Remembering
the night we swung our stolen swords

through crowded apartments in Alphabet City,
terrifying partygoers with impressions
of heat lightning, or Ohio when we climbed

atop holy rocks and whistled with the birds—
rapture cannot purchase, can only rent in my mind
which turns thoughts of rapture

to raptors, to swallows, to strep throat,
to tongue depressors, and the ascendency of 401(k)s
over pensions. What I want is to forget all jokes

and laugh like it was the first time. There are things
I wish I'd never seen so that I could see them again
and maybe this time savor them like a dessert.

What I'm talking about is *freedom!* though I could be
talking about chasing any high, love, or wildness,
each with their eroding returns. What I wouldn't give

for an afternoon in 2003, returning from a field trip
on a Friday in April as wet, bifurcated leaves
of Kentucky coffeetrees brushed the roof and sides

of the bus, and we were just forty-five minutes from home.
It wouldn't even have to be that moment exactly—
I just want another one that feels exactly like it.

Three-Day Weekend

Up there, it narrows from two lanes to one,
backing up traffic the whole way home,
but I don't mind. It's Friday before dark
and I'm in love with the world again,
from the opening bars of "Hotel California"
to the quality of the light at this particular hour,
this longest possible interval before being
thrust back to the working week once more.
The men and women who fought for our rest
wanted it this way: three days of freedom,
instead of two. Life is full of compromise—
we zipper merge, each vehicle ceding ground
to the next until we're a single line, the shadows
of trees and buildings passing across my eyes
like a zoetrope. A century and a half ago,
in Europe, my family's store was burned,
so they came to America and sold matchbooks,
their lives a testimony to the effectiveness
of their product. When I'm depressed, I feel guilty
for growing soft in relative comfort,
despite my ancestors' sacrifice. I don't even want
to look at the wreck that caused us
to come together, though it seems like a bad one—
splintered pole, downed lines, flashing lights.
No way anyone walks away from that.

Brighter Star

The drummer who beats dread into our lives
        has set his sticks on the end table.
Souped-up Camrys roar freely, bristling
        at speed limits and hastening
themselves along the beltway. Bats weave
        in the sky— a pair of anarchists
in darkness. This is as quiet
        as the night gets in these parts—
these immaculate machines at work.
        A neighbor wheels his garbage can
to the street and returns to the enclosure
        of his garage. I look up to the stars,
imagine holding one in my hand,
        like a single bulb in a strand. Magnificent.
And then I almost start to feel it burn.

Below the Dentist's Bent Arm and Through the Window, I See the Outline of the Shore Through Fog

He's trained with tools for decay
of a smaller scale, local erosion,
and I remember how much closer the end seemed
at the millennium: everybody's mother
reading apocalyptic fiction
by the pool while their children learned
to doggy paddle for their lives—
our computers wouldn't keep time
and I begged my parents to buy
canned food and water for the collapse.
Now the end is obviously closer
than ever and I have six hundred
TV channels to watch, and still
I choose the sad band on cable access
because somebody has to. Now some people
practice archery for the water wars
and pack their bug out bags, whereas some
of my friends are into reincarnation,
and think the future is fated in stars.
Some of my friends talk about Pascal's Wager
and others say there's nothing else behind the door—
bet it all on black—and some are already
through it—ones who carved pentagrams
into desks at the back of the class and gulped Xanax
in bathrooms all day—more through every year.
The end must be closer than then because
it is later now, and we are in the dark theater
where rats once darted about our feet
as they played the film of our lives,
and must we return in the lights?
And he says *we're all done now*, that I can
stop looking towards the shore, my mouth
now full of water and I spit it in the sink.

It's Morning Again in America

There is a lot of ruin in a nation and I am
the founding father of this one in particular,
pressing flesh for contributions at a donor breakfast.
Re-elect me, friends, and I will enact, on day one,
mandatory leave of soul from the body—
paid time off from the self guaranteed to all people.
And no longer will aircraft carriers lope beyond our straits with menace,
for we will be at peace, at last, I say. But the crowd
recedes from imagination, and I am hungry, thirsty, tired—

suddenly aware of a pain in my shoulder that makes me wince
when I remember it. Girls are bobbing like sparrows
in the plaza by the American Girl store,
cradling maroon bags, bracing themselves to welcome affection
into their hearts, and I ask a friend if he's ever felt joy like that.

Yes, he says, once, in Tempe, Arizona, in the '80s:
lying in the pool with a drink all morning, then tennis
then golf, then driving to the mountains and skiing all night
under lights. My friend and his roommate had the same racquet,
the same swing. *It was like playing my reflection*, he says. I can picture
it as he describes the muddled orange of the drink,
the gliding down San Francisco Mountain as an expanse of darkness

encircled it. Elsewhere, people were at rest beyond the beacon,
unconscious in their homes and therefore excluded
from description, a fate that once seemed worse than death.
The next day, my friend and his shadow piled
into their '65 Plymouth and returned to the valley, downhill
the whole way, no reason to even touch the gas.
All this wasn't only meant to impress you,
but the idea was always on my mind.

Contemporary Variation of the Flood Myth

I watch as not light but brightness
covers the dominion, blanketing first
a few patches and fragments, then connecting
as a lattice of touched-places until the break
is complete. God said to Noah "build an Ark
if you want to survive the flood" and so he did.
When God told me of the flood, I invented luxury
cruise liners so we could be more comfortable.
The vessels soon became dealerships trading in sin,
from the gluttony of buffets to that vulgar pride
inherent to boats—floating the way they do,
saying *I'd like to see you do this without me.*
I don't find the phrase "I need a vacation
from this vacation" funny because leisure is hard
when you're made to feel guilty for staying still.
But for a moment, I see it all. I look down from
the parking garage at the shopping center
and suddenly I believe in the Project
of the American Mall. I believe in the Beach Boys.
Everything below me is the color of bread,
and though there are many things I cannot afford,
they'd let me buy it all if I had the money.
If that's not a covenant, I don't know what is.

The Beach Boys

Sun worship just means being outside.

Something about
farthest sea adjoining sky
always makes me mourn the end of land.

Only once did I know peace at the beach—
finally following my mother
into the ocean on the last day
of vacation.

When the Beach Boys started
they mainly did a few kinds of songs:
I love cars and/or I love girls,
I love California. Then later,

fictional islands
that existed only in the mind.

As a boy I picked my scalp until it bled
and resisted sleep like a martyr
for the cause of waking.

I was born just before the end of history,
my life pure Apocrypha—
post-credit and non-canon.

The prevailing mode
of design in that time
was Global Village Coffeehouse—

earth tones and free trade:
wood, water,
and rope

adorning every vestige,
as if late-century abundance
were itself a product of whimsy.

The homespun gave way
to a barrage of images,
in malls,
homes, and restaurants—

distorted figures partaking

of life's largesse, in wine
snobbery and bagels,

carried on tufts
of steam
that scaled the sides
of mugs, the coffee therein

still imported
from abroad—
from actual places like Sumatra,
Honduras, Guatemala, Colombia.

And the old enemies were vanquished.
Turned into cartoons, too—
Gorbachev starring in Pizza Hut ads
and the Terminator
reverse-heal-turning good.

Today,
the rendered future is bearish
on existence, and more and more,
life feels
to me like running out

on the field at a baseball game—

emerging suddenly beneath lights,
usually nude,
then running until they catch you.

No two apocalypses are the same:
I sometimes like the beach
and the heat this time of year,
but it's hell
to wear the diadem of sweat

during eternal summer.

Shakespeare meant it metaphorically
as something fleeting immortalized in verse,

whereas I mean it more literally,
closer to the Endless Summer of surfers
who follow the season

across hemispheres. I have no new insights.
You have all the same information I do.
Even paradise is just a job.

Douglas Sirk Directs My Life

I have been as lonesome as the worst cowboy,
who, looking out across Wyoming, saw so little potential
for a state that he thought it might be better as a territory.
And yes, I have forgotten years of my life—there was once
a time that I couldn't envision a world without you.
What was the point of coming home unless I was
coming home to you—a commute past ballooning derricks
and the eerie silence of wind turbines revolving on the horizon.
I'm not talking about any former love—I'm meaning the chemicals
of derangement—in either case I'm being melodramatic.
When I was yours, the world unfolded before me
like a twinkling confection. If I could, I'd be reshaped
by the land and named by it, the way AstroTurf was named
for the Astrodome—the way Romans were named for Rome.

Whiskey Island

And so it happens that under the light
of a full moon and nearing 30, I am traipsing
through yards once more. It's not my fault alone.
It's partly a curse brought upon me by the man
who introduced wildness to our line—
whose bad behavior inspired an enemy
to light a cigarette at his casket
and blow smoke at his waxen face.
I myself am less charming than ten years ago,
when I skidded across the neighborhood's iced drives
with Jen and Joe, pursued by dogs,
our cackles filling the dark cul-de-sac.
Now she is married...now he is married
with a child and I am here, traipsing
through yards but older, fatter, knowing better—
a figure that mothers see in the dark
and recount in daylight to scare
their clean-cut sons. The night is silent
except for the crunch of frost-topped grass underfoot.
Smoke rises in the afterhours and an ancestral rascal
plays the burning piano in my ear.
O, calamitous things at work, wrack and ruin.
I have no son to teach a trade, no trade
to teach a son. Just stories of the man who bit
our apple. Who after closing the saloon,
saw an apparition of a woman
in a white dress walking along the crag
of Whiskey Island and vanishing into mist.
Now I stand at the end of my driveway
and look towards the neighbor's lawn, its twinkling bulbs
blinking in the hedges. All our standard ghosts are gone
and it's very quiet, except for the drip of ice becoming
water and passing through the storm drain.
Lord, is there any child of yours more treacherous than I?

The Passion of Saint Joan of Arc

We spent the best years of our lives living
above that sickly ravine.
Our heroes grew old and then so did I:

one by one, stomped like dauphins
in the revolutionary square, or, somehow
grew wings and took miraculous flight.

Upper lips firmed and facing the fire,
we drink of others and spread our disease
but they never offer us anything in kind.

Tell me, are there things in this world
for which you would die—when you
shut your eyes, tell me what comes to mind.

I am the duke of all earthly regrets.
I've made up my list,
and France isn't that high.

II.

Springtime; The Storm

Sunrise, first
torch. fresh motorcade:
day thawed

in the Capitol as roundabouts
lead us where we go.
All manner

of hornets buzzed.
This was spring then,
and warm in the shaded grove,

with rain wetting
my bones in a way
I'd always craved.

A classic truck, powder blue,
parked curbside—
opposite of airbags:

a metal steering wheel to cave
your chest at slightest
provocation—some blessed

gray day when everything
was in wane, lichens
sprouting like stubble, fronds.

It wasn't a dream, it was
a place. You were there. And you.

White Tower

Just before the promenade she turned
towards a chapel's yellowing sign
and said *maybe we should we just do it now*
right there on the deserted Niagara street,
still bereft of people on account of plague.
The city was still, as if an occupying force
had just withdrawn, and the mist plumed
in enormous columns, scaling higher
than the taupe casinos, the Rainforest Café,
or the Giacomo Hotel. In our room, I lay
in bed watching as dense fog eliminated the city
from sight. While she slept I swallowed
fiery thoughts. I shivered. I breathed. Anything
I could do to endure the fog so that maybe
the blinking tower could reveal itself again,
and then it did: its needle spire, its cascade of lights
signaling the existence of Canada, pouring in
through the hotel window
like theremin music through the dark.

Lunch in The Summer

—after Stephen Duck

The Lord is a painter.
Already he's retired certain colors—
set them aside to crumble
like the amusement park
on the edge of town,
gathering thistles.
But we still have green
in its many forms—
on lawns and boulevards,
under the noontime sun.
How I love lunch in the summer—
how good it feels to be allowed,
by law, to experience opulence:
sitting back in your car
in the Burger King parking lot,
food laid on your dashboard,
you become like a thresher
beneath a shady tree
three hundred years ago, scythe
nowhere in sight. Or, eating
a Caesar salad, you enjoy
the cool feeling of the porcelain plate
against your wrist and fingertips
as you graze it on the table.
Then it warms from your touch
and turns the temperature
of everything else.

Auto-Brewery Syndrome

Overgrown yeast in the gut can turn bread
in blood to wine. The body accumulates
a host of rewards for us when we do good,
and still, for gin, it usually just orders out
that ruptured compound that gives us joy.

Every drink I ever had was the second
to last one, meaning I meant it only once more.
I outlived Morrison, Keats, and Cobain.
The body, too, drafts legislation designed
to protect the ruling class.

January One

Dream of Jeannie. Dream of Dion
      and Bo Diddley. Of high and tights,
Hugo Boss, plimsolls and the VFW parking lot
      where my mother roller-skated as a girl.
At night I dream of Dayton—of oxidized bridges
      harboring graffiti like regretful tattoos
in intimate places. Of fireworks over the river.
      Of endless ranch houses with egg cream
vinyl siding and backyard basketball courts.
      I dream a horde of Catholic boys named things
like Tom and Drew to occupy those courts,
      then I funnel them all to Jesuit schools.
I dream I buy four ranch houses in Dayton
      and they become a hotel. I dream I pass Go

and inherit two hundred dollars. This morning,
      when I woke, I resolved to be more proactive,
so I left you to sleep. Last year's newspapers
      are flattened on the sidewalk by footprints,
stained by road salt: tell me, why is it I always
      tell someone I love them for the first time
on a Sunday, and do I always mean it as an apology?
      Today is the biggest Sunday if the week was a year
and I am still sorry. I believe this year will be different.
      I take a walk while the world is hungover,
everyone stirring sauerkraut at their stoves. I tell myself
      I feel better already and this time I believe it.

Travelers Insurance Presents: The Triumph of Man

Cheers to the first fish who ever felt wet
enough to stick his head out of the water.
Thanks be to him, the fishy father here
immortalized in museum display. I push

this button and let light fill the enclosure,
illuminating a tangle of ferns and volcanic rock
as this trailblazing fish takes the first steps
on stalwart legs. His cliff-faced progeny

harnesses fire in a cave down the hall—I push
a button and the room fills with the sounds
of crackling logs, the thudding music of bone mallets.
Now look here! What's this? Another display,

more glass partitioning me from Mesopotamians.
They drop boulders on raiders—in every room
there seems to be a fence, and in every room
there is a person climbing it. I approach

the New World wing: pioneers wave
from a passing barge. And on the right, the piled
corpses of Antietam. Each switch I flick
is like an apocalypse for another time.

The exhibit leaps forward to the brave aviators
taking aim for the stars—no mention of gas masks,
or trenches of the Somme, no amphibious landing
at Normandy. No mushroom clouds scaling the desert sky.

I follow the hall back to the atrium and think of
the spectators in 1964 who, upon emerging
from the red domed Travelers Insurance Pavilion,
found themselves once again in Queens.

Blessing for Wanderers

Loose me and let me go so that I am
carried forth by terrible squalls and taken
like this swarm of grocery bags is taken,
bounding across the blizzard like comets
against my whited vision. Let me be
liberated by winds like my neighbor's horde,
this polyethylene flock, and sent headlong,
submerged in the viperine streams and tributaries
of the world, yet with the grace of evening swimmers
who stride through darkness, glistening, flip-turning
eternally in the cerulean lanes
of the pool just below my window. And once
I am wrapped on a branch, or washed ashore,
grant me long stay and let me remain as refuse.

Tommy's Fever, 1997

It's like sending a letter to yourself,
the way after decades
a memory returns and you're subsumed
by ravine, bounded by leaves the color of canvas—

the air of that month a yellow cloud,
the delirious winds throwing branches.
And there's also the question of what
you were trying to prove to yourself—

what made you hold on to a memory so long
so that you could re-arrive at it, stumble
on it like a slot machine in dense forest,
on the casino floor of the carpeted earth.

Autumn Inventory

Another year, another harvest:
I am in a diner on 82nd Street
watching the children return
from summer, walking slowly,
adorned in back-to-school clothes,
and it feels as if the whole world
is a box of yellow pencils waiting
to be sharpened. And yes,
though they are returning to drudgery,
what a rush, still, to return triumphantly
someplace after months away,
to reappear taller and more mysterious,
like a deposed ruler they can't manage
to keep exiled. All that's left is to wait
for the first flimsy leaf to fall—
to unfurl from its tree like a smirk,
a remark which contains a slight against us
we've not yet been taught to understand.

Donkey Kong Country

As the wastrel son of a wealthy man,
like Chris Farley in the '90s, I'll do anything
to keep my father's company.
I'll make any grade, sell brake pads—
it's no difference to me. I was raised
to be polite, by which I mean compliant,
though rarely will I ever as a pedestrian
flash that little wave to drivers at the crosswalk
as if each Land Cruiser contained
an imperious Old Testament judge to grant me
clemency, safe passage to the other side.
I'm done groveling for modest courtesies—
thank you, sir, for not crushing me
like a dog right here in the street
beneath your chariot wheel. Thank you,
band of thieves, for choosing to rob another,
though I am an easy mark.
If I'm owed half a baby, I prefer top,
or better yet, recompense. Remuneration.
I myself was half a child and I turned out
stranger than the flock, lonelier. Poisoned
by the air, I spent a lot of time indoors,
a scion at a crossroads—reptiles had stolen
all the bananas in the land—my inheritance,
and it was my job to kill their king.

Denmark at Twilight

I am drinking in a bar called Denmark
that overlooks the convention center
when a man enters with his date, throws
his arms to their full length, gestures
across the expanse, and exclaims "Welcome
to my family's property." I try to imagine
the type of person who'd be impressed by this kind
of boast, though, to be fair, the date's not impressed.
She twists every pearl on her necklace,
shifting her weight as she says "Oh, wow!"
and they take the egg chairs next to me—
because this is that kind of place, you see?
The only time she doesn't seem bored is when
she's talking about the difference between
the US and Paris, where she lived for six months.
She tells him like a book report, so much that
when she's done, one might want to say:
Heidi, thank you so much for your thoughts on France.
Whenever I have thought about infinity
I have worried that it will feel like this—
like being left alone in the car at the store
with only your mind to keep you occupied.
Things should change. A man is given a watch
at the end of a career to mark his retirement.
A duckling becomes a duck and is covered
in plum sauce. I buy toilet paper no matter
what Romantic city I call my home,
and I'm sure that heaven will be no exception.

Reservoir

Here, they stock the lake with fish:
walleye, pike and bass, imported
to this place just to be caught.
The wake peels behind us—
surface unzipping beneath propeller
until the engine is cut
and we are carried on by the current.
Off the boat I'm almost weightless,

save for the tug of my ring
against my finger pulling me
towards the reservoir floor.
For your love, I am a swimmer.
You are what I envisioned
in all the time I was under.

Truth's a Dog

Why does it seem like
the last words
of funny fat men
are always "don't leave me,"
and why are they always
spoken to companions as they depart
in early morning? We're all just dogs,
set racing by the sound of the locking door.
We are Chris and John, and Chris,
and my grandparents' dog
Jester—four goldens now whimpering
at the prospect of solitude,
clattering brilliantly across
vinyl flooring every time
someone makes for the door.
It's dangerous for men to need
nourishment from others, but we are
dogs so it is our entire lives.
Somehow it feels more honest being this way,
capering in exchange for love.

Stay Boy

They never grow old in picture books. They just keep playing fetch across the page. And yes, someday the illustrator dies and gets replaced by his son but his son draws the boy and dog so much like the old man that you won't ever notice a difference. Boy and dog remain intact. They meet a cat and another time they go to the pool. The boy gets glasses. His dog licks him on his face—this makes the boy feel better but his glasses are gone by the next book and it appears that there is nothing at stake for the boy and dog. The ball rolls in the street but the car always swerves just in time. The boy visits a friend in the hospital but the book never says if the X-ray comes back with or without spots. The friend is never mentioned again, and, furthermore, the boy never takes a wife or a career in insurance. He never gets arrested at the park on a balmy night. And the dog never has pups with the Chow down the street. He never dies, gray fur and all, with the boy at his side. They never grow old in picture books. They just keep playing fetch across the page.

Meditation at Colonial Williamsburg

You should try being radiant,
little brother. You already tried glib.
Now stop treating life
like it's a game show you're hosting.
I have thought about you a lot,
about learning to swim in the guppy group

and the picture of the whale
unconscious at the bottom of the pool
in the swim safety class. A kid
drowned in that pool, you'll remember.
Hit his head on the ladder and sank.

In Chillicothe, they found a person
hanging from a fence by his sleeve.
Hours passed before they figured out
he wasn't a Halloween decoration.
If there's anything as pleasing
as its picture I can't think of it.

I've been thinking a lot about cake,
but not just any cake—there was
a picture book when we were young
that comes to mind. I believe it was
Go Dog Go. No cake has ever tasted
as good as that cake looked.

Lear Season

The gray and heavy rains of late
November roil against the roof,
knocking the shingles, frantic like a fist
against a locked out lover's door,
mid-quarrel: this is when the dog
decides he must go out to piss.
He prods the knob and looks to me—
his eyes opaque like marble taws,
both blind and filmed. He waits to hear
the click of leash upon his neck,

and so we wander through the yard.
Gloucester tugs at the line
wrapped around my hand, then blinks
in drops of rain and settles for
a row of pines, struggling to lift
his leg to mast. Afterwards he lies down
in the needle straw. He licks his paw.
Alright. *Let's go*, I say, and he replies
that we have seen the best of days.

III.

Please Wait While We Connect You with Someone

Some Sundays, after our large meal was through
and the counter wiped, my grandfather would sit in silence,
listening for hours to conversation as it passed him
around the table. *If I knew I was going to live this long,*
I would've taken better care of myself,
he would say, sometimes after not having spoken all day.
Only recently have I begun to seriously consider
his warning, or even allowed myself
to imagine leaving a better self for myself
to be collected in the mysterious future.
After a reading, someone once said to me: *No offense,*
but your writing is very nostalgic like it was a disease,
but I think of it more like the way you'd feel hanging
from a cliff by one hand and wishing you were hanging
with two. When a tow truck driver's killed in action,
tradition calls his fellow drivers to say *we'll drag*
the chains from here. Actually, the more I think about it
the more I resent being called nostalgic
when it's actually closer to the way a dog would bring
the entire tree home from the park if he was allowed.
I've spent my entire life collecting allegiances wherever
I find them—camaraderie in bakery lines, traffic jams,
waiting on hold to speak to a representative—
it's been a pleasure waiting with you all,
I say to myself as my comrades empty from the queue,
and a recorded voice says *there are currently*
four callers ahead of you. Until there are three.
Then two. Then one. We'll drag the chains from here.

Northeast Regional

I carry your words north with me
from New York to Boston,
my train tracing the coast
of Rhode Island, past the moored boats
that stare back at the shore
like a hundred hungry birds.
If I am the captain of my soul,
I am begging for a mutineer
to right this ship. All morning,
all the glass I saw was fogged—
bathroom mirror, storefront window.
No surface and the air could share
a temperature and I didn't see myself
for half the day. The city was the city
it had been when it had been my home.

New World

There was a sundeck at the edge of the earth
where we'd walk barefoot, throwing knives
into boards and we were truly careless.
We'd hang on the railing, looking out
at the highway that runs along the sundeck
at the edge of the earth, through the trees.
The earth is plausibly flat
if your sample size is small enough.

Walk Like a Man

—after Gary Snyder

The Four Seasons recorded "Walk Like a Man"
in a burning building. This is not a metaphor,
but it does cross my mind as I navigate a winding line

of high school football players, passing the unwashed
wide-outs, and tackles, the cornerback serving himself
another plate of food as our queue widens behind him.

That was my life, once: hurling my body towards another
to make him see stars, or to see stars myself,
because the creation of stars always requires pressure—

like a man in a hat in New Jersey who points a gun or a bag of money
at a DJ, who wields songs about teenage heartbreak
like the weapons they are, carving young men into spear tips

before our eyes, and to other tools, too, so they might be
useful to somebody some day. I have been thinking of tools
a lot, specifically the first one, a serrated stone that perhaps

aided in the sharpening of sticks, as each tool begets another,
like two hands swinging an axe to turn trees into axes
to break down the studio door they've locked themselves behind.

Contemporary Variation of the Flood Myth

Backstroke is the loneliest of the common crawls—
staring into light and girders of a pool ceiling,
submerging ears, milling our arms to propel
our bodies down the lane with no regard for grace—
these are the dances of capsized men.
Greyhounds pursue a rabbit around the track
and we too shall have incentive—a small picture
of a distant island that appears on our final lap,
and behind us, the smoke of a sinking destroyer
and the shipwrecked bobbing in waves as they fondly
remember every boat they ever set eyes upon.
I consider this as we stand drenched, huddled
beneath the ragged awning of The West End
like the ruined gatehouse at the edge of a walled city,
terminus before the water that ends Manhattan
and moats New Jersey. We are waiting for a deluge
to pass, though it snowed earlier today,
coming first in flakes, then as massive teeth
with ant colonies bored inside. Lounge patrons dwindle.
The sinks stay chipped. Light bulbs desert us freely.
All the old japes are passed. This must be how Arthur felt
counting empty seats at the Round Table. I wonder,
have I ever known a place that wasn't in decline?
I am Death's au pair: sent to watch his children
and learn the language in exchange for room and board.

Best Man Toast

I entertain a gentleman
at the bar with a factoid,
telling him that quinine
prevents malaria and he laughs
in my face. The dancers laugh
with him. The dancers tell me
my haircut is "Hollywood"
so I tip them. I try a new gin
with a different imperial mascot
each time. The betrothed
talks to the dancers while I drink
an elephant gin. The walls writhe.
I drink smuggled gin from
a flask and rehearse my best man
toast to a dancer. She claps
and I tip her. I tip the bathroom
attendant and drink a gin
with a wasp on the label.
I entertain a different gentleman
at the bar with a factoid
about insects: do you know
how hymenoptera—that's social
insects—tell each other it's time
to move the colony? They dance.

Easter

After the flood there followed draining, there followed
the first thaw—water receding, giving way to monstrous green,
massive walls of kudzu that overtook it all. I held you

on a hill of bentgrass where the crosses were rowed
beneath a sagging banner. Bunting remained from an old parade,
the way smoke lingers after the house is already burned.

I thought of another time in a shaded grove just before
the revolution when I was keeper of the king's roads—I set
a table and two chairs up in the wilderness and it was tamed.

Let It Go

My friend who works at Disney World
goes on vacations to Disneyland. He, like me,
prefers illusion to reality. And my great-grandmother, too.
In the '40s she saw her dead brother in the newsreel
before a film and wailed, overcome with emotion
in the theater—for a moment she thought
he might be alive after all. There he sat, projected
30 feet, laughing, smoking with other soldiers.
It didn't occur to her that the reel was shot months before,
or maybe she didn't care. All she knew was
he appeared alive. People joke that the movie *Frozen*
was named so that it'd be the first search result
for "Disney's frozen" instead of lurid stories
of Walt's head entombed in ice, awaiting reanimation.
We, the living, are always saying of the dead
I think he would have liked that about whatever things
we'd like them to have liked. A ventriloquist act.
The departed pass around us like a costumed cast
of our own theme parks, never seen without their heads,
and we choose to interpret that silence however we'd like.

Destiny

Khrushchev said the living would envy the dead
and here we are, escaping vapor
of a sublimated century—a dream stopped abruptly
by death in sleep. When I view the articles of my despair
after they've departed, I can barely recall
the person I was when I wrote despair into law—
very occasionally it's the dog who instructs the man to kill.
Call it role reversal. In high school I was in *The Glass Menagerie*
as the Gentleman Caller. It was the part I was born to play:
showing up midway through and failing to deliver
on even my modest promise. Everyone's waiting
on a tall stranger to come along to change their lives—
standing wistfully at the window long into the night,
waiting on someone exactly like me to appear and fix nothing.

Swan Dance

Tonight I watch a video of swans
reunited after being apart
and I am glad. We waltz along
the empty castle, singing

Happy New Year, baby, penniless
and wired, even though it isn't
the New Year, even though it isn't
Christmas yet, and just nights ago

I was in the ER with a fever
that wouldn't break, in the waiting room
next to a man who woke on occasion
to bellow threats at the staff. He held

his guts and rubbed his temples
at the same place where once
a great American tenor shot himself
with a BB gun and died six days later

because, he said, a wounded bird
cannot sing. After the waltz, we peek
from the blinds as a figure climbs
the construction site across the street

to the tallest point and lifts each cinder block
from a pile above his head like the Eucharist,
before letting them fall. When all the blocks
are in pieces, he climbs down and walks

off into the unlit alley, towards the squealing
friction of trains slowing on the tracks
at the place where an engine once derailed.
Life is just like prestige television:

ensemble cast, always changing, diminishing,
always replenishing until someone asks whatever
happened to so-and-so and the answer is always
that he died but no one ever remembers how.

The End of the Party

Is anything sadder
than the clearing room
at the end of the night?

Music suddenly
a little too loud,
the ice returning
to water once more.

It's the idea
of facing
daylight alone—

a beaming cop
standing
at your window.
Do you know
how fast
you were going
back there?

If I could tell you
I would.
I would say
anything
to have you
on your way.

Stooges

The saying goes "if you don't laugh
you'll cry" and though I do a good bit
of both I learned quickly
a person wears a joke the way
a man training dogs wears a bite suit—
both as armor and as a tool to train animals
the best ways to draw blood. My sister says
I look like John Hinckley Jr.,
Reagan's almost-assassin, and so I laugh.
When Reagan came to from surgery
from his gunshot wound he said
"Honey, I forgot to duck."
Of the Three Stooges, I always liked Curly best:
plump and guileless, impervious to harm,
like humor might save him, though it didn't.
Truthfully, he was a sad person playing
a much happier man, but the world
doesn't know what to do with that,
and what I want is to be in the world.
So what if the vampires who govern our lives
already won, and are on a victory lap?
So what if the air remains unfit to breathe
with our tender lungs? So what if the lungs
flattened are the size of a tennis court,
and still strain to make blood from dust.
If I laugh first I am, if not bullet-proof
then resilient, the same way the Stooges
sometimes ended a film all dead together,
plucking harps on the same cloud in heaven—
not forever, just until the next film.

IV.

Two Tickets to Paradise

I'm sensitive to the unique loneliness
of the state fairground forty-nine weeks
of the year, and the mall Santa in June,
and anything, really, that is an eyesore
out of its single context, returning me always
to the question "Is it better to be versatile
or to specialize?" Now I have everything
I want and still there is more to want—
the body is like a boat this way,
one that must be baled constantly to float
each morning as the swamp of light widens,
the darkness troughs, and I am stirred
from memory by an Eddie Money song,
"Two Tickets to Paradise," which describes
a literal vacation somewhere warm—two lovers
flying Delta down to Florida and drinking drinks
with umbrellas by the pool. They return
ten days later, tanned and telling
all of their friends how hard it was
to come back—wish we could have stayed forever,
Eddie sighs, steeping his tea as he exits
the break room. Before Groupon
was even invented, Ponce de León thought
that he might find eternal life in Florida,
which is different than paradise. And though
I know it's just a story that he was looking
for the Fountain of Youth, he dies in every version.

Bowery

A little girl practices kissing
on the window of a subway car.
Mwah, mwah. So what?
Her father's gold bracelet shakes.
He waves her lips from the glass.
And the Fillmore East is now a bank
with a wormy apple for a flag.

All the old joints are now spots.
Bye bye, Bowery. I walk into a boutique
and buy my baby boy a leather jacket.
Our tour guide says Basquiat ate a bagel
somewhere on this block. *So what?*

Bay Gulls

Whenever I see "Landscape with the Fall of Icarus,"
I hear this old joke in my head that starts
why don't seagulls fly over the bay, and then I wonder
if I'll ever understand art, or Auden at all. I don't consider
the way Icarus' legs are plunged in the water, nor the absence
of ripples they could have kicked. I never find myself
wondering where the schooners are headed. Instead
I am thinking how much Bruegel sounds like bagel, and then
a vision of the fog over Lake Erie on the day I heard the joke.
I can nearly see the flock—their wings flapping in time,
beating to keep white dough rings afloat above the mist,
sustained by illusion for as long as I don't think about the play
on words—a dozen bagels traveling as a V over a drifting barge,
slow as the continent, and they vanish past the city's last bridge.

The Two Gentlemen of Sandusky, OH

Midday in the tonsured city where even gulls
are stolen by wind: we have traveled miles

for the thrills, you see. To ride coasters,
and talk of love. And later in the French vanilla hour

before darkness expands like the barrel
of an accordion, and the swarming gnats come

to collide and couple in the air above our heads,
the coaster returns home. The bar is lifted

and we are giddy with the feeling of having survived
something once more, the high lasting long enough

to take us back to the A-frame before I want
to feel it again. So I say across the blackened loft

how I've been thinking of the days in the week
before I left for summer camp—how I thought I would die—

trying to eat ice cream on a Friday night, none of it
passing the lump in my throat. How miserable

I was worrying that I'd be miserable when I was away.
How I learned that this is the most important part of the game.

Aubade from Airport Cab

Two people on a stoop: the sun
begins to rise. She rests

her arm upon his neck and props
her head against his chest,

a trellis of tattoos, exposed and bare.
Then boats bouncing

in the harbor bay—
it's almost insulting how close

to the shore the boats all stay
when they could sail anywhere.

Pierogi Mountain

Born westward and early in the Decade of Nothing,
  prior to the reign of Good King Cobain
who died full of arrows before the century's end:
  that decade I almost drowned at the YMCA,

if not for the lifeguard who dropped me, still dripping,
  at the edge of the pool and left me alive.
Our neighborhood sat on a hill so they named it
  the Highlands, and called the streets things like

Angus Court, Loch Ness—any name generally
  considered Scottish was in play. From the window
I could see forsythia, burning bush, pink blooms
  of magnolias, and a private detective who parked

on the lane to watch a young wife return home midday.
  This was the Age of OJ, and one night in California,
Juice was taken by Bronco, his driver, Al Cowlings—
  in what they called a chase, but which ended at home.

Back in the Highlands, the people were succumbing
  to flesh-eating bacteria, ski crashes, flipped cars,
and midnight fridge raiders mistaken as prowlers
  and shot by their loved ones in unlit kitchens.

The young wife hired a hitman to kill her husband,
  but hired a fed and instead was arrested.
One spring we visited the Cherry Valley,
  but by then all of the orchards were long gone,

so the name remained as pure marketing, like when
   the ethnic neighborhood's been dissolved
into strip malls, and Little Slovenia Town sits next to
   the Market District, or Olde Fox Meadows long after

all of the foxes are killed. The town, called Worthington,
   was founded by James Kilbourne in 1803
and named after Thomas Worthington, because that
   was the Age of Thomas Worthington, a senator who lived

instead in Chillicothe, Ohio, whose name comes
   from the Shawnee word "Chalagwatha," given
to whichever place the chief lived at a given time.
   Colonists just pronounced it "Chill-uh-coth-ee,"

and it became the birthplace of wrestler Bobby Fulton,
   born James Hines in 1960, who wrestled in the '80s,
during the reign of King Terry Bollea, also known
   as Hulk Hogan. Neither Kilbourne nor Worthington

imagined the world after Hulkamania,
   the people terrified by stories of Lawn Darts,
the Satanic Panic, razor blades in chocolate bars—
   hysterical at the idea of *stranger danger*,

steering clear of sprinklers and other people's lawns
   because the neighbors had killed before and God knows
they might do it again. We were ready for a New Sensation
   (though this was after the Age of INXS), some small joy

to tide us while Class A office ziggurats declined to Class C
   and groaned off the sides of mountains. What could we do
except drink in parks under gauzy October skies,
   or in the carpeted walls of the Dolphin Lounge,

the cracked tiles of Café Bourbon Street, also called The Summit,
   also called Pierogi Mountain. After years of wasting
I am returning like Henry V, ready to receive my birthright:
   Joe steers the car down High Street, gesturing to the pile of bricks

where The Library stood, and we are like Al and Juice, again,
   one man keeping another in motion so that he might flee
from thunderous music. But no, in truth we are not Al and Juice.
   Not Hal and Falstaff. He is Lot and I am his wife in that moment

after she turned but before she was changed. I am salt
   in a meadow and the ground is a crater beneath me,
and someday the people will buy homes in a place realtors call
   Salt Creek Ravine, long after I'm gone. Any name just holds a place.

Terminal

In dreams, I live beneath a grand glass dome roof
so that I can view the elements and never
face their danger. It's the oldest story,

really. For tonight I sleep on the floor
of my sister's bungalow, burrowed
in burgundy shag carpet and I am warm

for the first time in a while.
As in some nineteenth century novel,
I have been sent here to collect my sister.

Worse, I have come to her straight
from a Catholic funeral in Appalachia
for a death so unexpected I borrowed pants

for the wake. The wood-paneled walls
buckle and shift from the passing storm,
and when it's time to sleep, that's the time

I take inventory of my sins. My life
has been a sequence of desperate acts
in the service of being wanted. I lie awake

and draft unimpeachable defenses
for my personality, knowing that one day
I will have to answer for myself.

Going to sleep always feels like watching
a lover pass through TSA and vanish
into the terminal. Solipsistic inventions—

eyeballs squirming, cooking up pictures
which beget nothing and fade in waking.
I don't want to sleep because I want to be

awake with all of you more than I want
to be alone. I don't want to dream because
I always miss everybody. I admit it.

Women of Oncology

Neon fish circle the surface of the tank,
pursing lips at the sunken flakes of food
as Carol the nurse shuts the lid. Elsewhere,
a doctor administers Thalidomide,
among other drugs, to my grandmother,
who sits with her hands clasped in a vinyl chair.

The women of oncology are in bloom—
are in blue scrubs, rolling across the nurse's station
to file the charts of another week. A medical assistant
places a folder in a drawer labeled hospice.
They talk about a barbeque on Sunday,
who all will be there. Then, when the poisons

have run their course, Carol returns
for an attestation: *Are you able to become pregnant?*
Do you understand that Thalidomide is proven
to cause birth defects in gestating fetuses?
and it's strange to me that they're asking this now
when it's already over
and the drugs are at home in her blood.

No Call, No Show

I was scheduled to work on the apocalypse. It had been predicted by a preacher who said the end was coming that day. He had said it a few different times, actually, before landing on that particular day. I wanted to stay home but my boss said "We need you. Come in or you're fired" so I went to work. The golf course was packed with a hundred men ready to die doing what they loved, or a hundred men who hadn't heard about the prophecy. It was impossible to know who was in what category. Actually, that's not entirely true—the golfers who thought the end was near were never so generous, and gave me lots of tips. They wouldn't need cash where they were going. By dusk the course was quiet. Thunder rumbled in the distance. A cellophane yellow haze hung over the last light. I set a folding chair at the door and waited.

Lemon

—for Max Ritvo

One fine day, some lemon
got away from his bag
and rolled intractably under

a Subaru, where no voice
could summon him home.
And beneath this Subaru he had

all he needed to grow by way
of dirt and water. And had he not
been a lemon in New York City,

where the streets are swept
twice a week, he might've
come up a tree. And he'd have grown

through the car, provided the Subaru
never had to move; provided he got a bit
of sun. In another life he will be a pine.

Scientists will count his rings to study
his years: did it rain often?
Was it a time of plenty?

Pax Romana

For a time I felt harmonious and whole,
if you know what I mean. Ringing bells alone

could make a Christmas and when I climbed
the red rungs of the fire tower to survey the tree line,

no smoke was visible on the horizon.
Every good despot remembers things this way—

that stretch of time that precedes the pageant's end.
Before is always better, but I am not indiscriminately

nostalgic. I always know when a moment will be mourned
while it's happening. And along came a discordance,

something that broke me thoroughly, irreparably,
you might say, the way objects forged from a single piece

can never be fixed, only patched. And patched I am.
Isn't it strange straddling these two centuries the way we do?

When I was young I was in love with "Wanderer
Above the Sea of Fog." Now I have claustrophobic dreams

of trying to push through the crowd to the doors
of the train, and wandering through the Gap,

looking for chinos in that length but this color,
and do they have it in the back, which I'll never know

because I leave to catch the last train back to waking
before Dream Clerk returns from the stockroom.

Nowadays, I think I'd like to see that painting's face,
to name those mountains. I've grown to like specifics.

In Coshocton, Ohio there's a roadside attraction
called Unusual Junction—an old depot famous

for housing the original sign from The Price is Right,
autographed by Bob Barker. I can picture it now:

the mass of light bulbs, a blinking incandescent dollar sign
in the depot just as an archipelago of clouds

begins its procession around the moon, and below,
the closest thing to moorland in America lies still.

The foothills of Appalachia take shape in the distance,
giving way to steep mountains that drape the continent's breast

like a sash carved from 500 million years of glacial drift
and tectonic collision. I knew then that I would remember

the splendor of the moment, as I do tonight, sitting
on a balcony in Newport News, Virginia, bitten repeatedly

by mosquitoes—the buzzing, swarming little shits—
as they come from the marsh below this apartment.

I swat at them casually, as if they weren't responsible
for killing more humans than any other thing in history—

as if right this moment they weren't spreading malaria,
West Nile, Zika. Our ancestors were passed over

by mosquitoes like a final plague, leading me here to Virginia,
sitting on this porch staring across the dark at the farm where all day horses

ambled in the pasture. An orange Sunkist machine glows next to a barn,
so startling and gorgeous that I had to travel here to experience it,

beneath the din of every insect in the marsh calling out for a mate.
I am here because of my discordance. I am here because mosquitoes

let my ancestors live, allowing me to travel to this remote peninsula,
and there are worse places to be exiled. I look to you, strange machine

in the dark, and paraphrase Virgil when I say that one day I'll come
to remember even this moment fondly, when it is completely behind me.

Matinee

A stagehand bumps the flimsy wall and the poem collapses
like a house around Buster Keaton. Who in this room
needs to apologize for artifice? I do. Maybe it's that, for years,
I slept with the television on to drown out obsessive thoughts.
Life flipped before my eyes like a magazine, so now I'm here
staging one-act plays for the empty house. The stagehands
wheel the stucco buttresses away and begin to strike
the set. Each Potemkin Village is torn down
and carried off into storage. I have always been this way—
always lonely when the credits rolled. I'm not ready to leave
just yet. I stick around the theater, my feet kicked up
over the seat in front of me, my cigar still burning, leaving piles
of ash in the aisle. Houselights go up and I see the speckle
of confetti across the proscenium. An usher sweeps the debris
that remains, leaving me and my ash. When the usher's gone
I'm the last one left in the poem, and I'm a little afraid
to be here without anything else to distract me.

ACKNOWLEDGMENTS

The author thanks the journals in which the following poems previously appeared or are forthcoming, including:

The Atlas Review: "Bowery"

Baltimore Review: "Three-Day Weekend"

Booth: "Below the Dentist's Bent Arm and Through the Window, I See the Outline of the Shore Through Fog"

Cider Press Review :"Truth's a Dog"

Cleaver Magazine: "Pax Romana"

DIAGRAM: "Springtime; The Storm"

Epiphany: "Best Man Toast," "Aubade in Airport Cab," and "Brighter Star"

EuropeNow: "Feast of St. Michael and All Saints," and "Blessing for Wanderers"

Grist: a Journal of the Arts: "The Two Gentlemen of Sandusky, Ohio" and "It's Morning Again in America"

The Kenyon Review: "Whiskey Island"

Mississippi Review: "Contemporary Variation of the Flood Myth"

Muse/A Journal (*Birdcoat Quarterly*): "Terminal"

The Night Heron Barks: "Easter," and "Swan Dance"

Open Space: "Lunch in the Summer"

Pine Hills Review: "Denmark at Twilight" and "Walk Like a Man"

Rust & Moth: "January One" and "Freedom!"

The Scores: "Auto-brewery Syndrome" and "Lear Season"

The Shore: "Meditation at Colonial Williamsburg"

Sixth Finch: "No Call, No Show"

Southeast Review: "Contemporary Variation of the Flood Myth"

TYPO Magazine: "Douglas Sirk Directs My Life"

ABOUT THE POET

Christopher Blackman is a poet from Columbus, Ohio. His poems have appeared in *The Kenyon Review, DIAGRAM, Cleaver Magazine, Southeast Review, Booth, and Epiphany,* among other publications. Former co-host of the podcast *Poem Party,* he received his MFA from Columbia University, and has been an instructor for the Kenyon Review Young Writers' Workshop. He was a finalist for the National Poetry Series, and a semi-finalist for the Autumn House Press Poetry Prize. He currently lives outside of Boston and works at Dana Hall School, a 5-12 Day and Boarding Girls School in Wellesley, Massachusetts.

More from Gunpowder Press

Before Traveling to Alabama, poems by David Case
Mother Lode, poems by Peg Quinn
Raft of Days, poems by Catherine Abbey Hodges
Original Face, poems by Jim Peterson
Unfinished City, poems by Nan Cohen
Shaping Water, poems by Barry Spacks
Mouth & Fruit, poems by Chryss Yost
The Tarnation of Faust, poems by David Case

California Poets Series

Downtime, poems by Gary Soto
Speech Crush, poems by Sandra McPherson
Our Music, poems by Dennis Schmitz
Gatherer's Alphabet, poems by Susan Kelly-DeWitt

Alta California Chapbooks
Emma Trelles, series editor

On Display, poems by Gabriel Ibarra
(selected by Francisco Aragón)
Sor Juana, poems by Florencia Milito
(selected by Francisco Aragón)
Levitations, poems by Nicholas Reiner
Grief Logic, poems by Crystal AC Salas

BARRY SPACKS
POETRY PRIZE WINNERS

2023

In the Cathedral of My Undoing, by Kellam Ayres
selected by Gary Soto

2022

Accidental Garden, by Catherine Esposito Prescott
selected by Danusha Laméris

2021

Like All Light, by Todd Copeland
selected by Lynne Thompson

2020

Curriculum, by Meghan Dunn
selected by Jessica Jacobs

2019
Drinking with O'Hara, by Glenn Freeman
selected by Stephen Dunn

2018
The Ghosts of Lost Animals, by Michelle Bonczek Evory
selected by Lee Herrick

2017
Posthumous Noon, by Aaron Baker
selected by Jane Hirshfield

2016
Burning Down Disneyland, by Kurt Olsson
selected by Thomas Lux

2015
Instead of Sadness, by Catherine Abbey Hodges
selected by Dan Gerber

Printed in the USA
CPSIA information can be obtained
at www.ICGtesting.com
CBHW030204140324
5326CB00002B/94

9 781957 062129